NO MAN'S LAND

Kathryn Southworth

NO MAN'S LAND

© Kathryn Southworth

First Edition

ISBN: 978-1-913329-25-9

Kathryn Southworth has asserted her authorship
and given her permission to Dempsey & Windle for these poems to be published here.

Published by Dempsey & Windle
15 Rosetrees
Guildford
Surrey
GU1 2HS
UK
01483 571164
dempseyandwindle.com

British Library Cataloguing-in-Publication Data

A catalogue record for this book is available from the British Library

Acknowledgements

Part 1: Many thanks to John Lucas for his advocacy of Ivor Gurney's poetry and his kind help with this project.

Part 2: A first-hand account of Whiteway can be found in Joy Thacker's book *Whiteway Colony: The Social History of a Tolstoyan Community* (1993).

Without Adrian Davis I might never have visited Gloucestershire — and certainly not made it my home.

Cover illustration

The starting point for the Ivor Gurney poems was the series of memorial windows in Gloucester Cathedral by Tom Denny. Many thanks are due to the artist, to the photographer James O. Davies and the Chapter of Gloucester Cathedral, for permission to reproduce the detail of light 7.

Other works by Kathryn Southworth

Someone was here, Indigo Dreams Publishing, 2018
Wavelengths, (with Belinda Singleton) Dempsey and Windle, 2019.

CONTENTS

Part One:
Bright tracks where I have been: poems for Ivor Gurney

Part Two:
No Man's Land: a verse drama set in a utopian community

Part 1: Bright Tracks where I have been: poems for Ivor Gurney

The songs I had are withered
Or vanished clean,
        Yet there are bright tracks
Where I have been.

Ivor Gurney, '*The Songs I Had*'

1. And may Gloucestershire guard from all sorrows

I searched a churchyard by the road
that leads away from town
toward the orchards and the fields
that spread out all around.

Do not forget me quite, O Severn meadows

And to the east rose Cotswold edge
keeping its watch across the plain
where great St Peter's tower thrusts
its tracery of stone.

Do not forget me quite, O Severn meadows

And there I found a marble slab
all white and glittering in the sun,
but set amid the tended graves
it seemed a sad and lonely one.

Do not forget me quite, O Severn meadows

So finding an unkempt straggling verge,
I snapped two poppies that were almost done
and laid them on parched earth before the stone —

one for the Severn and one for the Somme.

2. What shall please the wind?

We are making a new world on the Somme,
for order, peace and freedom to break through.
But what shall please the wind now the trees are gone?

Fritz will bury Tommy when he's done,
he'll mark him with a cross, give him his due:
we are making a new world on the Somme.

But where did the wood to make a cross come from,
here where the planes are splintered and askew?
Oh what shall please the wind now the trees are gone?

Those planks the soldiers walk upon are numb,
those beeches that once on Crickley blew,
for we are making a new world on the Somme

so men can sing free as larks when war is won,
and all the promises of peace made true,
but what can please the wind now the trees have gone?

The blasted trunks gesture to the sun
as if the heavens could be appeased and wooed.
We are making a new world on the Somme
but what shall please the wind now the trees are gone?

3. Squaring

Virtue lies, you said, in making squares,
the order of Roman camps and roads.
Odd, from one who shirked the tidy life,
set hours, regular meals, those tyrannies,

yet studying the intricacies of Byrd and Bach,
loving the solidity of the great cathedral tower,
you volunteered for army life and all
that discipline of drill and endless cleaning,

and despite your obstinate odd versifying,
elisions, strange syntax, crowded lines,
you stuck with rhyme and metre, just about,
as if you feared the consequence of letting it all out

without restraint of river bank —
that Dionysian tide
that floods the Severn valley
and sweeps everything aside.

4. Gap-mender

Music was clearer to you,
seeing the hedger weaving
such patterns of bright green;
thought left behind
by certainty of fingers
so quick and sure,
was reason to envy —

this narrative needed no plotting,
the mind didn't see what the hand did.

But I, no country child to learn from lore,
could not find it for myself directly
nor in the lovely intricacies of Bach,
then, only in literature,
marvelling with Lawrence
at a snake or peasant,
imagining the secret was
in Etruscan sun, Mexican blood —
some lifestyle further off
or some past art —

that might heal that breach
of head and heart.

5. Ventriloquists

It saved your life, no doubt of it,
that noble fool officer's soft language —
Do you think you could crawl through
that uncut wire towards certain death?
Not likely! You'd have thought,
I don't think so, sir, you said.

You mimicked him so well,
civility and common sense prevailed.
You weren't above studied ventriloquy,
revelling in the language of the squaddies,
the lyric warmth of the Welsh lads —
your ear was sharp and sound.

It's women, they say, lose
their own language soonest,
adapting to interlocutors.
I'd winced at my sister's self corrections —
the long southern *a* taken for *bath*
the way she said the colour *m-o*-ve for mauve,
but once I'd learned to pronounce the proper $\underline{u}$ in *cup* —
(an Indian living in the US taught me that)
I wasn't really northern any more or working class

and, if it saved my life
or saved from anything at all —
I'm not sure what that was.

6. Mariners

Restless, you haunted the dockside,
sidling up to the ships' captains,
begging to be taken on, to reprise
contentment of soldiering's physical work,
the mental release of obedience.

They knew better.
Perhaps it was the gleam in your eye,
your hands were soft, or maybe your language,
they caught in you too much whiff of land —
or the word just got round

that the organist at the Mariners' Church
poetiser with friends in London,
fancied being a sailor;
so the grey walls of chapel and its bleak
commandments were as far as you got.

By then, Blighty was no longer home —
or too much like that draper's shop and dreary street
you'd walked away from all your life before,
unhappy mother, put-upon brother.
You found family elsewhere,

but like a cat gone roaming,
easing itself into neighbours' houses,
coming back from time to time to sniff its bowl
or curl up in the best chair, you never quite lost touch,

and she never quite gave up on you, Mother,
despite the shame of her mad son
and the 3d she paid out each week
for the Gloucester Journal you never read.

7. Gloucester

You said untidiness would all be smoothed away,
respectable red brick rule all,
no small shops of multi-miscellany.
Did you imagine the sprawling shopping mall,
designer outlets where the dock warehouses stand tall?

There'll be no football in the streets, you thought,
or chatting at front doors.
But how could you foresee
the new communities that gather here,
the hallal butchers, Polish grocery
crowding out uniformity.

And the centuries that drape this city
still lend a mellow grace,
Roman foundations set in glass pavements,
friaries uncovered, even
the fictional tailor and his Simpkin given their space.

All gleaming in that special light
where town meets country
and country runs out to sea,
here, as if new risen from the water,
Mistress of the widening river.

8. Ways of the world

Ivor disputes with Ronald Gurney

First dream, a little stone Cotswold house
in a small valley, cool grey and green,
and guests to bring news
of the great world and its goings on.

Then a wanderer, Wycombe to Gloucester,
not settling to any job —
cinema organist, post-office clerk —
sleeping in hedgerows, singing for pennies,
harming no one, he said, this way of life.

Enough drifting, wrote Ronald,
just make a bit of an effort!
Forget you're someone special!
Think of others as well as yourself!
Learn a little discipline!

And maybe he had a point.
Can all of us harbour our dissidents,
shrug off that daemon the Protestant ethic,
live for the moment?

So I walk past the beggars in the street,
knowing for some — though which? —
this is a choice, of sorts, an opting
out of taxes, the daily trudge to work.
Give a token instead
to the charities that take them on,
being like Ronald,
another *rank and file compromiser.*

Though things might have turned out differently
for me, too — denying responsibility,
job, house, pension.

I think
of the way not taken.

9. How goes it with the hills?

Malvern your touchstone for the day,
darkly purple across the valley's broad rift,
mine a domestic dawn, east from the Cotswold Edge,
knowing the other side Painswick stream
better than this one —

how goes Bull's Cross today, Longridge, Sheepscombe?
Jigsaw pieces with my house the centre,
gathering up lower hills and ridges,
with its purse string.

Inside we can see nothing.
Day starts when I close the door
and turn the corner to look out.
There.

Today the slopes are mizzled,
hunkering down under heavy clouds.
Yesterday was crisp and clear, sun
catching that strange chalet roof
below the escarpment topped with woods,
mid-centre of the sheep-stoned pasture.
Tomorrow, maybe, heat-haze.

Morning seen and gone,
there is no other like it —
each the only one,
and each day light is changed forever.

10. *What use is vassal breath that lengthens pain?*

Gone out each every bright thing from my mind,
me exiled from familiar woods and hill,
smoothed out and ironed flat and filed.

I search for memories, but nothing living can I find,
my word hoard spent, no joyful showers can refill,
since every bright thing is gone out from my mind.

Here there are only lawns to roam and walls to climb,
safer for me and those who brought me here, until
my world is smoothed out, ironed flat and filed.

So let them bring their needles, I'll be mild
and meek and subject to their will,
since every bright thing is gone out from my mind.

The twilight world to which I am consigned
would better be erased, be whited out and still,
this life that's smoothed and ironed flat and filed.

They show me books they say are mine —
too late — the poems that I wrote are bitter pills
since gone is each and every bright thing from my mind —
smoothed out and ironed flat and filed.

11. Helen Thomas visits Ivor Gurney

He met me in pyjamas and a dressing gown
but there was nowhere in that bare room to sit down.
I put my flowers on the bed, no vase —
glass or pottery shards can sever arteries.

He liked the pretty hat I'd chosen specially to wear
and stared directly in my face
as if he sought a likeness there
to my dead Edward. *Let us talk of him*, I said.

In the common room was a piano
and Ivor played — but none of the men
who sat around, eyes bent upon the floor,
gave any sign they heard.

He wouldn't go into the garden — that travesty
of countryside. If only he were let
out to his Gloucestershire for an hour's happiness…
What if he did end his own life after that?

So next time I brought Edward's ordnance survey map,
and Ivor trod those lanes and villages again,
with finger walking down each track,
better than ever we sane could imagine them,

wandering the hills beside my husband,
though they had never met — and Edward
brought back to life for him
and me.

12. Absence

The wind whimpers, wanting me
as it wanders across my little hill.
The river is winding to the sea.

The sun will play over the grass and tree
and the days stretch out their hours, until
the wind whimpers, wanting me.

Once I would walk through the night and still be
up when the sky thrills with the lark's trill,
now the river is winding to the sea.

Gloucester was all mine, valley and lea,
far Malvern and purple of Cotswold sill,
but the wind whimpers wanting me.

Silver at midnight and gold as honey
the city I homed to and swayed to, still,
as the river is winding to the sea.

There's no one can help such a one as me,
punished by unending exile until
the empty wind whimpers, wanting me,
as the river winds to the sea.

Part Two: No Man's Land

A verse drama set in a utopian community.

1. Whiteway

Find your way to the roof of Gloucestershire,
beyond the handsome stone of Painswick,
past mellow Sheepscombe, pretty Miserden,
through avenues of beech and larch
to the back-of-beyond,
and you may stumble on a onetime white road,
on either side shacks and bungalows
dumped anyhow.

This was The Colony.
And so it is still.

Gathering all conditions of folk,
from university to able seamen,
and many women too,
giving a most picturesque effect
with bare legs and heads,
feet covered only with the sandals of the ancients.
(Postcards of this quaint scene
may be purchased in Stroud post office.)

Living, at start of their new life,
by Bible rules, all held in common
without coin or any law but conscience
brotherly love and free union,
and small and grown up people just the same
called by their Christian names alone,
brothers and sisters between them all.
Close to the land and what the earth produces;
for want of matches they rose with the sun
to bed at sundown.

No sugar, salt, no bread
but grain ate raw in the hollow of your hand.

There were no artists then
but all were artists.

2. Declaration

The idle rich dress every day
as if they were on holiday

Moths and vermin will destroy their treasure

They do not cultivate their soil but live
on those bowed down by illness and despair

Blest are the meek, they shall inherit

The idle love their horse and carriage,
estates and tithes and others' labour

He will pull down the mighty

Theirs is the land who work it,
as right to share as sun and air

Salt of the earth, we pledge never to own it

3. The Applicant

To the Secretary. Whiteway, May 1913

Dear Comrade, seeing an account in the Daily Herald,
has filled me with desire to join your colony.

My wife and I are socialists, out and out,
and want to quit the town, anxious for a good start
in life for our little son of four years old.

Tailoring is my trade and my wife, by profession, teacher.
though we would take up any work
of benefit to the Community.

We are vegetarians and in good health.
Yours fraternally.

4. Bonfire

The faithful all lived together and shared everything in common.
— Acts 2.44

Forty-one acres at seven pounds apiece are theirs —
or not — as the collective vote decides
on who can settle, those that think as they themselves,
with no rules written down, no rights and wrongs
save trust alone. And yet deeds must be signed
for land to be exchanged.
Who is to do it?

The chosen ones
are Joe, Sinclair and Sud
selling their souls for the common good,
honour saved by treating pitch with pitch,
the papers spiked on farm forks, smeared with paraffin,
then set alight, the ashes left to scatter to the winds,
no trace of compromise — not yet.

The common house might give way to new separate homes,
the wash house used no more, its copper left to cool,
the wringer rusty, when people have their own roofs and water buts
and finally water comes to everyone in pipes at last.
But principles are principles — they share the costs
to make sure each of their individual toilets flush
and workman are invited to a special celebration,
their boss, Harry, wearing a dicky bow that twizzles
like an aeroplane propeller,
for they know how to throw a party.

Come their jubilee, they write mock deeds
to burn upon a bonfire by the ceremonial beech tree
and baker Protheroe makes a birthday cake
weighing a full twenty-five pounds,
fifty candles flickering in the Colony Hall
in the glare of the new electric lights.
where their communal pot of cash still graces the
mantlepiece.

5. Liberty and Free Love

Who can go through the eye of the needle?
Sam Bracker, maybe, he who agrees
to give away his fortune for the cause

They shall declare his righteousness
for he tried to keep his promise
and was sore tried

Blessed are the pure in heart
for their intentions are good
though life sometimes gets in the way

And the greatest of these is love
Love conquers all and when you fall in love
you must keep something back for your family

Blessed are the merciful
but when others fall in love
their misdemeanours may require a letter to the newspapers

Casting the first stone
and the righteous man may need
four police man with him to argue his case

Set your light upon a hill
Sam speaks — more in sorrow than in anger —
"win over neighbours by example, not by scandal"

Thou shalt not covert thy neighbour's oxen
Except when they are bought with your hard cash —
Sam doesn't claim the land, only the cows on it

What's in a name?
The cows are yielded up,
no longer *Primrose* and *Leap Year*, though,
but renamed *Liberty* and *Free Love*

6. The Major General Investigates

Intelligence is required on this collection of subversives,
rumoured Bolsheviks, who would not hesitate
in offering assistance to the enemies of their nation
already known to harbour dissidents, draft dodgers,
anarchists and foreign aliens, smuggling criminals away,
proclaiming the British Empire an oppressive occupation force,
flouting the law on registering births and deaths,
branding all regular order illiberal officialdom,
holding marriage nothing but a shackle on free union.

Not just the usual misguided intellectuals and dreamers,
they have some solid citizens in their number,
bank managers, business men and such, pillars of the community
abandoning their collars and very decency,
flaunting their bare legs and feet and going naked bathing,
a serious affront to passers-by.

We seek a man and wife to infiltrate this rabble
and bring back hard evidence of wrong-doing
enabling action to be taken to rid this country
of the enemy within.

7. Manners Have They None

A month we lasted, among their visitors,
attending tedious lectures to avoid detection,
living on stew and stew and stew again,
bare-headed and only sandals on our feet,
skin turning brown and hard.

Since they have no requirement of holy wedlock
which they regard as shackling by officialdom,
slave morality demeaning to the female sex
who must relinquish names and freedoms,
and be labelled as men's property,
they practice *promiscuous fornication.*

We can say no more, but our report is this:
that manners have they none
and their customs are most beastly.

8. Released

Never serve any military service, for war is sacrilegious to the divine man.
— Leo Tolstoy

They arrived by motorbike,
Tom from Pentonville,
Lillian from Holloway, complete with newborn —
three months each for printing and distributing *Defying the Act.*
Their press followed, occupied the Carpentry Shop.

Lillian's day job was in Stroud
in charge of the Sunshine Health Food Stores,
leaving each weekend to edit *Freedom.*

Britain was too tame for Tom
who left to save the Continent, running *Italian Libera*,
whilst Lillian hung on in to save humanity itself
marched on Aldermaston, relishing arrest.

Died, aged 98 in Cheltenham.

9. Nooitgedacht

No names at first once they'd agreed
to separate houses, just bare descriptors —
Bungalow (despite an extra storey now),
Sinclair's Hut, Red House, North End.
Then they got more poetic, though still rooted in reality —
Woodview, The Rowans, Meadoways.

Sud's bricks, made from the stream's free clay
moulded and baked, never quite took off.
The wood and glass for Sunnymead cost thirty-seven pounds ten
and came on a lorry sent from Birmingham;
but Francis Sedlake built it all himself
and it still stands, only the roof raised just a bit.
Then there's *The Croft*, made out of bacon crates
shipped from London, and the railway wagon
(Great Western Railway company, of course)
brought in by Hugo Van Wandennayer for his family
and named *Nooitgedacht,* Dutch for *Would you believe it?*

Not all harmonious. Take George Barker's garage.
Wrecking his three-wheeler Morgan car on Lecky Hill
George got it home to scrutinise it indoors — using a candle.
Conflagration.
He dragged away the twisted mess of blackened car
to save his precious garage
which, having no use after that, was deemed by the community
a derelict eyesore to be removed forthwith.
When George refused, five colonists were deputed
to do the job themselves. George complained to the police
and the five were summoned to the Petty Sessions Court at Stroud,

which deemed the issue was beneath its notice.

10. *Alan Did*

Let no opportunity go to waste.
When Cranham Sanatorium is auctioned off
the Colonists are there and in three weeks
dismantle the building with its wood verandas
and reassemble it at Whiteway – it takes three years,
kitted out with soakaway, earth closets and urinal,
roof oxide-red, windows and doors ultramarine,
as they still are.

It's booked up every evening and weekend
for lectures — three hundred and forty-one of them,
like *The Unconscious Mind*, *History of Russian Literature*,
The Female Organ of the Plant — and folk dance, drama
group, recitals on the new grand piano and, most important,
classes in Esperanto.

For the world has come to Gloucestershire —
Gandhi himself is to visit —
and the Communal Holiday Home, in its first year,
hosts two Samalis, a Zulu, a Chilean,
a Japanese, German, Russian and five French.
This is the brainchild of Eugene ('Gassy') who recovered from TB
furthered his social anthropology
with a ten year World Tour, by bicycle and foot.
He names the guest house in the universal language —
Alan Did.

11. Snip, Snap, Snob and Chip

I have told of fellowship
and you have harkened and understood

The cloth our weavers spin
Snip makes up into suits
to dress outsiders in.

When Adam delved and Eve span
who was then the gentleman?

There is no boss in our Workshop.

We'd rather walk to London
even through the snow
than use the postal service
and pay those we don't know.

We'd rather jail than taxes.

But maybe Snob, the sandal man
and Chip who works the wood
won't shame to sell to allcomers
their surplus goods.

Together we'll pay out tithes.

And Snap who takes the photographs,
record our story right
so children will remember
and keep the message bright.

Now is the time appointed
in which you may, if you will,
cast off the yoke of bondage,
recover liberty.

12. I Kan Ryme of Robin Hood

Letter to the Colony Secretary

Two years I lived free and joyful, making my own house of wood,
cultivating my allotted land, thriving in the common good.

Two years I lived watchful and full of regret,
llstening to rumours, pondering, insecure,
here is the cause …

Ye ben wastours I woot well

It's the water gone from Will's rain butt,
from Peter's plot cabbages missing,
fruit disappeared, potatoes lost from Hodge's
and a colonist seen searching the nests of my breeding birds.

A hard word, *steal,* I cannot bring myself to use it,
can't bear to send this letter, reach that brink.

But ye been wastours I woot well

These things are generally known between us
and no steps taken.
What is mine, is yours, we'd rather say.

But time has come for me to think again
and some place else
about what kind of life might be for the good

and if Robin Hood ever in greenwood stood.

13. The Challenge

Then shall no man mow the green grass for another
and he who builds a house shall live in it
with those that he bids share it of his own free will,
and fellowship will be established in heaven and upon earth.

The pioneers were set against all legal processes
until a settler went to law in nineteen fifty-five.

Your own lands you till, unless some cursed lawyer
dressed in sheepskin, should steal it from you.

The case was heard in London.

Since olden times (well, AD 1200), the Courts said,
land tenure law allowed that all together could be licensees
of their own land, their monthly meetings establishing the lore.

Case dismissed.

The Colony Secretary came home to a surprise party.

But most of the fifty-two there
felt sorry for the settler, a lady of advancing years,
who'd lost her case and costs

and would not let her pay, bearing it all themselves
as small price for vindication of the cause.

It waved about our infant might
when all ahead seemed dark as night.
It witnessed many a deed and vow,
we will not change its colour now.

Notes: Part 1: **Bright Tracks where I have been: poems for Ivor Gurney**

1. *And may Gloucestershire guard from all sorrows*

The title and refrain echo lines from Gurney's poems *What I will pay* and *Song.* 'Poet of The Severn and the Somme' was the way Gurney badged himself.

2. What shall please the wind?

The title and repeated line are taken from Gurney's poem *Possessions.*
We are making a new world is the title of the WWI painting by Paul Nash owned by the Imperial War Museum.

3. Squaring

In *The Motets of William Byrd* Gurney suggests the composer's quality is evident from the manuscript page alone with the 'master' of 'square-making'. In *Compensations,* speaking of poets, he says 'virtue lies in square-making'. Presumably he is alluding here to stanzas.

4. Gap-mender

This poem is a response to Gurney's *The Hedger.* My father had some of the country lore celebrated here but I was, as Gurney puts it, 'more used to book-poring than bright life'.

5. Ventriloquists

This poem is a response to Gurney's *The Quiet One.*

8. Ways of the World

See Michael Hurd, *The Ordeal of Ivor Gurney* for correspondence on this early dream and letters from Ronald Gurney.

9, How goes it with the hills?

This poem responds to Gurney's *poems The Touchstone* and *Yesterday Lost.*

10. *What use is vassal breath that lengthens pain?*

This poem draws on Gurney's *Sonnet September 1922* but repurposes his original phrase 'What use to vessel breath.'

11. Helen Thomas visits Ivor Gurney

This poem draws on the account in *The Ordeal of Ivor Gurney,* taken from a memoir by Helen Thomas written for the *Royal College of Music Journal,* 'maps' evoking the visit by Helen Thomas'. Tom Denny's window in Gloucester Cathedral depicts these maps scattered round Gurney's feet.

Notes: Part Two: No Man's Land: a verse drama set in a utopian community

1. Whiteway:

This poem draws on early accounts of Whiteway in the *Stroud Journal* and the memoir of the 'little waif', Sophie Carman in a letter of 1914.

2. Declaration:

This poem intersperses sayings of Tolstoy with the *Sermon on the Mount* and the *Magnificat.*

41

6. The Major General Investigates	Source — The Public Records Office, MI5 Director of Intelligence Major General Sir Wyndham Childers
7. Manners Have They None	The italicised phrases are taken from the official report. No evidence was presented.
10. *Alan Did*	*Alan Did* is Esperanto for *Flag Ignorer*
11. Snip, Snap, Snob and Chip	The principles of early Whiteway are interspersed with sayings attributed to the hero of the Peasants Revolt, John Ball.
12. I Kan Ryme of Robin Hood	The title and italicised lines are taken from *Piers Plowman Passus V and Passus VI.*
13. The Challenge	Verses in italics are based on Morris, *The Dream of John Ball*, Langland, *Piers Plowman* and James Connell *The Red Flag*. James Connell was a visitor to Whiteway. This sequence as a whole draws on the account of Joy Thacker: *Whiteway Colony: The Social History of a Tolstoyan Community.*